THE FIVE-MINUTE
HORS
D'OEUVRE

THE FIVE-MINUTE
HORS
D'OEUVRE

JOAN MOSS

With many thanks to Phyllis Ennes of Anacortes, Washington, for her invaluable help.

Text and illustration copyright © 1993 Breslich & Foss

Conceived and produced by Breslich & Foss, London

Photography by Nigel Bradley
Illustrations by Marilyn Leader
Designed by Clare Finlaison
Original design by Lisa Tai

Published by Crown Publishers, Inc., 201 East 50th Street
New York, New York 10022.
A member of the Crown Publishing Group.
Random House, Inc. New York,
Toronto, London, Sydney, Auckland

CROWN is a trademark of Crown Publishers, Inc.

Manufactured in Hong Kong

Library of Congress Cataloging-in-Publication Data

Moss, Joan.
The five-minute hors d'oeuvres / Joan Moss.
p.   cm.
Includes index.
1. Appetizers.   2. Quick and easy cookery.   I. Title.
TX740.M638 1993
641.8′12—dc20   92–30667
CIP

ISBN 0-517-59265-7

First Edition

CONTENTS

THE FIVE-MINUTE APPROACH

Hors d'oeuvres, whether a preliminary to a sit-down meal or a meal in themselves, are excellent social ice-breakers. They are informal and relaxing, and their variety, presentation and decoration can often be the subject of conversation before tongues have loosened up for gossip, scandal or serious discussion. To encourage this, hors d'oeuvres should be small, attractive in appearance, intriguing in taste, and – as one hand is usually occupied with a glass – easy to handle.

Hors d'oeuvres should be presented contrasting each other in appearance, texture and taste, and in enough variety to give guests the pleasure of plenty of choice. They will look attractive served on decorative plates, but care should be taken that the dishes do not detract from the hors d'oeuvres themselves. With more elaborate pieces it may be better to use a white plate. It is also important not to over-crowd – not only do hors d'oeuvres look more attractive when well spaced, they are also easier for guests to pick up.

Factors to take into account when deciding how many hors d'oeuvre pieces to prepare are: (a) how substantial each one is – a stuffed olive on a stick is very different from a puff-pastry bouchée filled with rich potted crab, (b) whether they are merely appetizers, with a full meal to follow, or an end in themselves, and (c) the types of guests invited – young men usually eat (and drink) much more than elderly ladies. As a rough guide, you could expect each person to eat between five and fifteen pieces, depending on the circumstances, and you should prepare about five different types for ten guests, increasing to seven types for twenty. It is probably better to prepare too many than to have too few, but on the other hand not many hors d'oeuvres will keep until the next day, so left-overs are likely to be wasted.

Savories from the supermarket

When you are very limited for preparation time, even five minutes may be more than you can spend on every recipe, so it can be a good idea to supplement the more elaborate canapés with simple savories straight from the supermarket or deli shelves.

The recipes in this book have been devised with five minutes preparation time in mind, and have been made easy enough for the most inexperienced cook to serve a tempting and tasty assortment. Although you might find that making and decorating hors d'oeuvres becomes such an enjoyable activity that you could spend hours in their preparation, this is not really necessary, and a dramatic and elegant effect, much appreciated by guests, can be achieved with the minimum of time and skill.

EQUIPMENT
It is not essential to have all of the equipment mentioned here, but it will help to achieve 'five-minute' hors d'oeuvres. The majority of the items will be standard in many kitchens.

Hand tools

Knives. A 3 inch (7.5 cm) paring knife, a 6 inch (15.5 cm) cook's knife, a bread knife and a finely-serrated fruit knife are essential. A finely-serrated, curved grapefruit knife is useful too, for hollowing out vegetables, such as cucumbers, before filling. A 3 – 4 inch (7.5 – 10 cm) palette knife is the most convenient tool for spreading soft fillings on bases.

Kitchen scissors. These are often more efficient than knives for many jobs, such as snipping herbs and trimming bases to shape.

Chopping boards. A large chopping board, heavy enough to provide a solid working surface is essential.

Basins. A number of these will be needed, from a large mixing bowl to smaller basins, if several hors d'oeuvres are being prepared. A measuring jug can double up as a bowl for whipping small quantities of, say, cream.

Spoons and spatulas. A range of these in stainless steel, flexible plastic and wood, in various sizes, is important for mixing the fillings and assembling the hors d'oeuvres. A small fork for mashing small quantities of ingredients will also come in useful.

Sieves. Metal or nylon sieves are good for draining ingredients such as shrimps (prawns) or mussels. More flexible than a colander, they allow effective drying from underneath, using paper towels.

Baking trays. Hors d'oeuvres cooked in an oven will need a baking tray. A pair of tongs for turning items in the oven or under the grill will avoid burned fingers.

Graters. The square stainless steel variety is best as it is easy to handle and has several grating surfaces, ranging from fine to coarse. Many have a slicer for fruit or vegetables. A potato peeler can also be useful for cutting thin slices of vegetables for use in decoration.

Piping bags. Nylon bags with several sizes of plain and indented nozzles are essential for speed when filling and decorating hors d'oeuvres. (See p.13.)

Cutters. The cutters normally used for pastry are useful for cutting round, toasted bases. Smaller ones (truffle cutters), in various shapes, are very useful for making decorative pieces from thin slices of vegetable or fruit.

Pitters. Olive and cherry pitters are the quickest way of removing the pits from small fruit, and are essential if pitting has to be done in any quantity.

Larger equipment
Apart from the refrigerator, freezer and microwave (used mainly for defrosting) which will probably be standard equipment in most modern kitchens, a toaster, an electric blender, a food processor and a mixer are essential when speed is the primary aim. A mechanical slicer, can be extremely useful for uniformity, particularly with bread-based hors d'oeuvres, where slices are sometimes needed from the longest side of the loaf and are harder to cut evenly.

All equipment should be ready for use close to the work surface if its time-saving facilities are to be used to the greatest effect.

HORS D'OEUVRES BASES
The main purposes of bases in hors d'oeuvres are: (a) to add a contrasting taste and/or texture to the filling, and (b) to make a firm foundation for the filling so that it is easier to handle. Some hors d'oeuvres, however, are small and firm enough to be eaten directly from a cocktail stick without the need for a separate base.

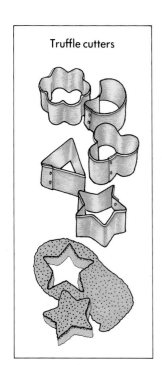
Truffle cutters

Carbohydrate bases

bouchée cases	pita bread	tartlet cases
bread	pizza bases	toast
crackers	pumpernickel	toasted wafers
croustades	rye bread	tortilla chips

Toast is the only one of the bases which must be made immediately before it is needed. It can be spread with butter (or substitute) on one or both sides, before or after toasting. A long French stick cut across in rounds is very suitable, and is a change in taste and texture from ordinary white or wholemeal bread. In addition to bread, any supermarket will also offer a wide variety of crackers – round, square or triangular – which can be used to vary the size, appearance or taste of the pieces.

Some pastry bases can be bought ready-prepared (usually frozen) from supermarkets and delicatessens, but when these are not available you will always find packs of un-shaped puff and short-crust pastry for making your own. Bread croustades, tartlet and bouchée cases (puff-pastry shells) are more unusual hors d'oeuvres bases which you can easily make at home.

Bread croustades
1 Remove crusts and roll out bread to ⅛" (3mm).
2 Cut to 2½" (6.5mm) squares. Brush both sides with butter.
3 Press into muffin tins. Bake in a moderate oven for 12 minutes.

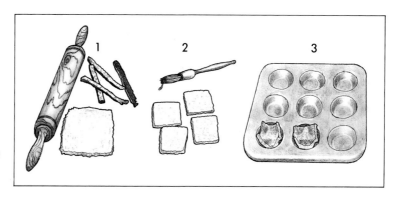

Tartlet cases

1 *Roll out pastry to ⅛"*
(3mm). Cut with a round
cutter.
2 *Line tartlet tins with the*
pastry and prick bases.
3 *Line with wax paper*
weighted with beans. Chill
for 15 minutes. Bake in a
moderate oven for 10
minutes (removing paper
after 5).

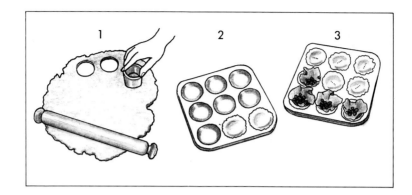

Barquette cases

1 *Roll out pastry to ⅛"*
(3mm). Cut into ovals.
2 *Press into barquette tins*
and trim the edges. Line with
wax paper and beans. Chill
and then bake in a moderate
oven for 10 minutes.

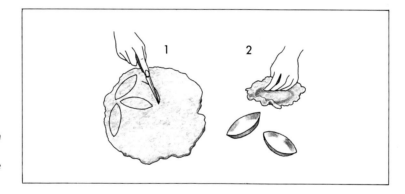

Bouchée cases

1 *Roll out pastry to ¼"*
(6mm). Cut with a round
cutter.
2 *Make an impression in the*
center of each round with a
smaller round cutter.
3 *Chill and then bake in a*
moderate oven for 10
minutes. Remove the centers.

Fruit and vegetable bases

artichoke hearts	dried apricots	prunes
celery	mushrooms	sweet peppers
cucumbers	palm hearts	tomatoes
dill pickles	potatoes	yams

STORE CUPBOARD
For last minute hors d'oeuvres, and to save time, it is always useful to keep some ingredients in store.

Cans

anchovies	frankfurters	salmon
artichoke hearts	mussels, plain/	sardines
asparagus	smoked	scallops
baby corn	oysters	tomato purée
clams	palm hearts	tuna
condensed soups	pâtés (a variety)	water chestnuts

Jars and bottles

chutneys	ketchup	soy sauce
gherkins, cocktail	lumpfish roe	Tabasco
ginger, crystallized	mayonnaise	walnuts, pickled
herbs (a variety)	mustard	Worcestershire
horseradish	olives	sauce

Fresh herbs are infinitely preferable to dried.

Packets

crackers	nuts, whole/	parmesan
dried fruits	chopped	potato chips

Freezer

bouchée cases	shrimps	smoked salmon
crab meat	(prawns)	tartlet cases

Refrigerator

cheeses, hard/	eggs	yogurt
soft/blue		

Fresh

fruits	meats/fish,	vegetables
herbs	cooked/smoked	

If the cooked or smoked meats are bought in vacuum packs they will keep longer, but they will have more flavor when freshly cut.

DECORATION

Hors d'oeuvres must not look as if they have been made in five minutes, even if they have. A little extra decoration can make a lot of difference without taking much time. Some of the recipes, such as stuffed eggs, are naturally decorative and need very little extra garnish; others are more neutral and are much improved by attractive colorful touches of fruit or vegetables, cut into shapes.

Fancy piping

One of the most useful tools in assembling and decorating hors d'oeuvres is the piping bag. For putting the main filling into, or on, the base, a plain nozzle about ½ inch (1.5 cm) in diameter is normally adequate, but for piping decorative mixtures such as savory butters or cream cheese, a finer fancy nozzle will produce the best results.

Piping bag and nozzles

Garnishes

Carrots. Very finely grated carrot can be used as a bed on the plate or as a border on the hors d'oeuvre base itself. Very thin slices of carrot can be cut into fancy shapes with truffle cutters, or into small plain circles with an apple corer.

Pimentos. Green, red or yellow peppers can be cut into strips or shapes, and their vivid colors stand out particularly well against dark fillings. They are especially effective when cut into shapes with truffle cutters.

Radishes. Small radishes can be used just as they are, with the tail cut off and some of the greenery left on top. With a little more time, radish roses can be made.

Peas. Snow peas (mange-tout), blanched and whole, make a vivid splash of green on oval or rectangular hors d'oeuvres. They can be cut and combined with peppers or tomatoes, or spread on a plate like the petals of a flower with a round hors d'oeuvre placed in the center.

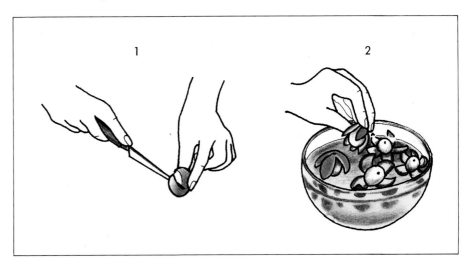

Radish roses
1 *Cut petals of red skin round the radish, from root to leaf, leaving the base of the petals uncut.*
2 *Place in iced water for 10 minutes.*

Tomato roses
1 *Starting at the base, peel a thin strip all round the tomato, to the stem.*
2 *Place strip flat, flesh-side down. From stem end, roll up skin to form a coil.*
3 *Put flower on its base and fold in last piece of skin to form a more open petal.*

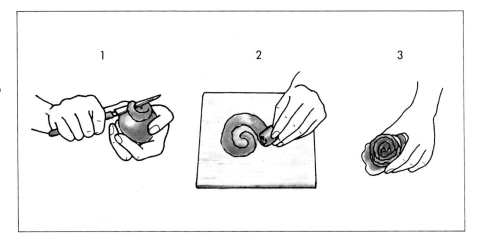

Citrus fruits. Lemons, limes, oranges and kumquats are invaluable, as there are so many ways they can be used. Thin slices can be used flat or, by cutting from the center to the outer edge, made into cones. Thicker slices can be halved or quartered and stuck into the filling so that the colored rind stands out above it. Narrow wedges can be used in the same way.

Olives. Black or green olives, when pitted, are often cut in half lengthwise for garnishing. The pimento-stuffed green olives are cut across so that they present concentric rings of red and green. If served on cocktail sticks they can be stuck into a base – perhaps half an avocado, pitted, and placed cut side down.

Tomatoes. Medium-size or cherry tomatoes can be cut in slices horizontally across the fruit or in thick or very thin wedges. When more time is available a tomato 'rose' – on a bed of thinly-sliced cucumbers or blanched snow peas (mange-tout) – makes a spectacular decoration for a place center (see above).

Eggs. Hard-boiled eggs are not only a standard hors d'oeuvre in themselves when stuffed, but can also be used for decoration when cut up or chopped. A classic garnish used by French chefs is 'mimosa'. Cooked egg yolk is forced through a fine sieve so that it resembles the ball-like clusters of mimosa flowers. Parsley and cooked egg white are chopped together to make the 'foliage'. This is not a five-minute decoration, but it is unusual and attractive.

Herb flowers. These are among the most striking and comment-provoking garnishes, but unfortunately are available only in season and depend upon your having a garden for the plants. The small, vivid blue borage flower with its dramatic central black spike is perhaps the most striking and useful, as the plant has such a long season. Borage will grow in almost any soil and one plant will provide hundreds of flowers. The blossoms of chives, rosemary, thyme, sage and nasturtiums are also very effective. It is best to stick to the flowers of herbs as so many other flowers are poisonous.

Garnishes from cans and jars. It is worth looking round the supermarket or deli shelves for things that can be kept in store for garnishing, such as capers, gherkins, anchovies, maraschino cherries and cocktail onions.

Herbs. Almost anything you have can be used, although parsley (curled or flat), chervil, dill, fennel, sage, tarragon, chives and basil are the most useful. If you do not have room to grow your own, most supermarkets now stock a good selection of fresh herbs. They can be chopped and sprinkled on the top of mixtures or used in small sprays. If after buying them you wash them, place the stems in a jar of water, cover with a plastic bag and place them in a refrigerator, they will keep fresh for up to two weeks. They must be well dried before you chop them or they will stick to the knife and to each other.

Nuts. Most varieties of nut can be used as garnishes: almonds (raw or roasted, whole, chopped or slivered); cashews; pistachios (for a green color); macadamias; walnuts; pinons (pine nuts).

TABLE DECORATIONS

Hors d'oeuvres are sometimes carried round on trays, but if they are to be displayed together on a table, it is worthy of decoration. Flowers are an obvious choice and, when in season, herb blossom (especially those mentioned above) make excellent and appropriate posies.

More unusual are 'flowers' made from vegetables. In addition to the radish and tomato 'roses' mentioned under 'Garnishes', above, carrots can be used to make an attractive centerpiece. Long strips of carrot are cut using a potato peeler. The slices are dropped in boiling water before being curled and secured in a base (see below).

Another vivid orange 'flower' can be made by sticking kumquats on cocktail sticks and securing them to sprays of glossy evergreens in a vase. Radish rosettes can be displayed in the same way.

Carrot flowers

1 *Cut carrot lengthwise into fine slices and drop in boiling water for a few seconds. Drain and dry.*

2 *Coil strips and secure with cocktail sticks in a potato. Conceal with greenery.*

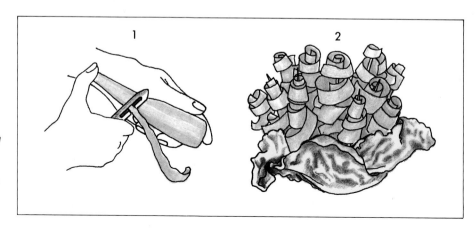

TIME-SAVING HINTS

- Before you start, make sure everything is on hand – can-opener, chopping-board, knives, piping bag and nozzles, etc. It is useful to open all cans and jars before you start.

- Take ingredients out of the freezer and refrigerator well in advance, to make sure they are ready for use – butter softened, for example.

- Have herbs ready.

- If you are making hot hors d'oeuvres put some wooden cocktail sticks in water to soak for several hours so that they will not burn under the grill or in the oven.

- If you are making a large number of items, process in bulk anything you may be using frequently – slice vegetables; chop ingredients such as ham in a food processor; boil all the eggs you need, shell them and keep in cold water.

- When piping flavored butters and cream cheeses use several bags and nozzles, filled with the most-needed ingredients. The easiest way to fill the bag is to fit the nozzle first and then place the bag in a beaker, folding the top of the bag over the rim. Spoon in the filling. Pipe as usual, replacing the bag in its beaker after each batch.

- Making toasts individually can take a long time and you may find it worthwhile to do them in bulk. Buy an unsliced loaf and cut it along its long side, discarding the crusts. Spread sparingly with butter and then toast. When cold, spread the whole slice with the filling mixture, and cut into shapes with a knife or cutter. Each canapé can then be decorated or finished individually.

Quantities: the ingredients given in these recipes will make at least ten of each hors d'oeuvre.

1
IMPROMPTU
HORS D'OEUVRES

CELERY AND CHEESE DIP

Ingredients
8 fl oz (240 ml)
  condensed cream of
  celery soup
4 oz (100 g) blue cheese
2 oz (50 g) Leicester, or
  other crumbly hard
  cheese
1 Tbs Worcestershire
  sauce
1 Tbs crystallized
  ginger, chopped
1 stick celery
salt and black pepper

Dips, perhaps thought of as a product of the twentieth-century cocktail round, have, in fact, a far longer history – and the same problems in eating them persist. In 1356 Geoffrey Chaucer in *The Canterbury Tales* said of the fastidious prioress,

> Nor dipped her fingers in the sauce too deep
> But she could carry a morsel up and keep
> The smallest drop from falling on her breast.

The secret then, as now, is to make the 'sauce' thick, so that it clings to the dipping pieces, and then to make a quick transfer from dish to mouth.

Serve with sticks of carrot, cucumber, peppers or other suitable vegetables, or cereal-based dippers such as corn wafers, bread-sticks, or toasted pita.

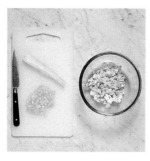
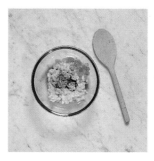

1 *Crumble the cheeses into a bowl. Stir well and add the celery, finely chopped.*

2 *Add to this the cold soup, Worcestershire sauce, ginger and seasonings, to taste. Stir together well.*

3 *Pour into serving bowl and surround with sticks of vegetables, fruit, breadsticks and crackers.*

ANCHOVY AND CHEESE WAFERS

Ingredients
10 toasted wafers, 1½"
(4 cm) square
1 × 2 oz (50 g) can
anchovy fillets
2 oz (50 g) low fat soft
cheese
1 tsp Dijon mustard
1 Tbs brandy, or ketchup
pitted black olives, for
decoration
dill sprigs, for decoration

The taste of anchovies on their own is too salty for many people – in this recipe it is mellowed with a mild-flavored cheese. Dijon, the mildest of all mustards, is mixed in while the brandy (or ketchup, if preferred) helps to smooth the sharper, more dominating flavors. The number of fillets you use will vary from two to six, depending on your taste and the strength of the anchovies.

Anchovy fillets are not very easy to mash, but if they are snipped into small pieces first they will mix in with the cheese fairly readily using a fork.

Because this hors d'oeuvre is still quite strongly flavored, it should be served in small amounts, and the toasted wafers which can be bought commercially are ideal for this – there is a limit to the amount you can pack on 1½ inch squares.

The black olive rings are an unusual garnish and add a sharp clean flavor which complements the earthy anchovy-cheese mixture.

1 *Mash together the low fat soft cheese, anchovies and mustard.*

2 *Add brandy (or ketchup) to make a stiffish mixture.*

3 *Pile a heaped teaspoon of mixture on each wafer and decorate with slices cut from the olives, and dill.*

SARDINES AND TOMATO

Ingredients
1 × 4 oz (100 g) can of
  sardines
2 Tbs tomato purée
2 Tbs cider or wine
  vinegar
1 Tbs mayonnaise
10 salted crackers
cucumber, for decoration
cherry tomatoes, for
  decoration

Sardines are said to derive their name from Sardinia, where they have been caught in vast quantities from at least Roman times. They are now caught worldwide, and though most countries claim to have the finest, the French maintain that theirs, caught in the cooler Atlantic waters and lightly cooked in oil before being packed, are superior to any others.

Many tinned goods deteriorate with age, but within reason sardines seem to improve, the flavor becoming more mellow. The most expensive are packed in the finest olive oil, but many canners use sunflower, cotton-seed or ground nut oils.

Traditionally, sardines are served on toast, and toast can certainly be used in this recipe, but salted crackers make a pleasant change.

1 *Mash the sardines, tomato purée, vinegar and mayonnaise together, with a little oil from the can.*

2 *Cut slices of cucumber about 1/8" (3 mm) thick and small sections of cherry tomato, for decoration.*

3 *Pile the sardine mixture on the crackers and then decorate.*

POTTED CRAB BOUCHEES

Ingredients
10 cocktail-size bouchée
  cases (see recipe p. 11)
6 oz (150 g) fresh, mixed
  crabmeat
1 oz (25 g) butter
1 egg, beaten
2 – 4 Tbs single cream
1 oz (25 g) Cheddar
  cheese, finely grated
1½ Tbs brandy
pinch of cayenne pepper
salt and black pepper
thin slices of lime, for
  decoration
parsley, dill or fennel
  sprigs, for decoration

The soft creamy mixture of the crab, piquant with the addition of the cayenne and brandy, contrasts well with the crisp flakiness of the pastry in this recipe. Packets of ready-prepared bouchée cases may be available, or, in some supermarkets, the frozen, uncooked ones. Home-made ones from packets of frozen puff pastry also give good results – see recipe, page 11.

If you can get it, fresh crab has the the best flavor, and it can be bought ready dressed. When crab is out of season, the frozen meat is a good substitute, but cans are not really suitable because they often contain only the white flesh, which lacks the flavor of the brown meat.

The lime cones used for decoration are made by thinly slicing a lime into rings and then slitting each slice from its center to the skin. The edges are then overlapped. Push the cone into the crab mixture, and finish off with a sprig of green herb.

1 *On a very low heat, melt the butter and cook the crab in it for about a minute.*

2 *Stir in the egg, cream, cheese and cayenne, and cook gently. Stir in the brandy.*

3 *Remove from the heat. Taste, adjust seasoning and fill the bouchées.*

4 *Decorate with lime cones and herb sprigs.*

TUNA AND GINGER TOASTS

Ingredients
3 medium-thick slices of
  bread, 4" (10 cm)
  square
½ oz (15 g) butter,
  melted
4 oz (100 g) canned
  tuna fish
4 Tbs natural yogurt
1½ Tbs crystallized
  ginger, chopped
cocktail cherries, for
  decoration

Tuna fish is a standard, deservedly popular, ingredient of hors d'oeuvres, but when it is just piled on a cracker with an olive on top it can be rather bland. It may seem unlikely that two such differing flavors as tuna and ginger should blend so well, but the chopped ginger gives a very unusual 'lift'. Stem ginger in syrup, which can be bought in Chinese specialty shops, is an unusual alternative.

The maraschino cherry is mainly for color, and other bright garnishes such as red pepper shapes, red cocktail onions or halved cherry tomatoes can be used instead. The flavors with these will, of course, be very different.

Toast is a particularly good base for this filling, but it should not be made too long before eating. If the hors d'oeuvres stand for several hours the juices from the fish and yogurt may soak into the bread and make it soggy.

1 *Brush one side of the bread with the melted butter, and then toast.*

2 *Drain the tuna and mix together with the yogurt and chopped ginger.*

3 *Cut the toast into 1½" (4 cm) circles and pile some of the mixture on each.*

4 *Scatter chopped chives over the tuna, and place half a cherry in the center of each piece.*

SMOKED MUSSELS IN TARTLET CASES

Ingredients

10 tartlet cases (see
  recipe p. 11)
4 oz (100 g) smoked
  mussels, canned in oil
3 oz (75 g) butter,
  softened
1½ Tbs tomato purée
4 tsp paprika
juice ½ lemon
salt and black pepper
dill, parsley or chervil
  sprigs, for decoration

Fresh mussels are not always available, but most supermarkets have the smoked, canned variety that goes into this unusual and intriguing hors d'oeuvre. A 4 oz (100g) can usually holds 30 mussels.

When arranging the mussels in each tartlet case, place three in the shape of a triangle, leaving a space in the center for a rosette of the butter and tomato mixture, or a sprig of greenery.

Use an icing bag with a small star nozzle to pipe the mixture. Swirl a rosette in the center and then pipe a ring round the edge of the tartlet. To contrast with the tomato-red of the mixture, decorate the rosette with dill, fennel, parsley, chervil or, as here, with celery leaf.

If this hors d'oeuvre is made in advance, brush the cases lightly with a little melted butter before filling, to keep them crisp.

1 *Beat together the butter, tomato purée, paprika, lemon juice and seasonings.*

2 *Drain the mussels and place three in the center of each tartlet case.*

3 *Pipe on the butter and tomato mixture, and then garnish.*

Eggs stuffed with curried ham

Ingredients
5 eggs, hard-boiled
2 oz (50 g) boiled ham
1 Tbs chutney
2 tsp curry powder
1 Tbs chopped chives or
    scallions
1 tsp paprika
salt and black pepper

The combination of ham and eggs is so delicious in all its forms that it is difficult to go far wrong with it. In this recipe the addition of curry seems to enhance the flavor of the egg, and the chutney lightens the texture of the ham.

When hard-boiling the eggs it is important not to overcook them, as the yolks may become too hard and develop an unsightly green ring. To avoid this, cover the eggs with cold water to which has been added one teaspoon of vinegar, and bring to the boil. Simmer very gently for ten minutes – the water should scarcely move. Remove the eggs and put under cold running water for 30 seconds. Shell them when cool and put into cold water until needed.

To decorate, add a light sprinkling of chopped chives or scallions and a dusting of paprika to give a touch of color.

1 *Halve the hard-boiled eggs lengthwise and force the yolks through a sieve.*

2 *Chop the ham finely and add it to the sieved yolks. Add the chutney and curry powder.*

3 *Combine thoroughly. Add seasoning and pipe the mixture into the egg halves.*

4 *Sprinkle lightly with chives, or scallions, and paprika.*

2
COCKTAIL PARTY
HORS D'OEUVRES

SMOKED SALMON ROLLS

Ingredients

2 slices brown bread,
  6" × 5" (16 × 13 cm)
5 oz (125 g) thinly sliced
  smoked salmon
¾ oz (20 g) softened
  butter
1 – 2 tsp creamed
  horseradish
lemon juice, to taste
freshly ground black
  pepper
chives, for decoration
2 sheets wax paper

The flavors of smoked salmon, brown bread and lemon blend so perfectly that this is a classic hors d'oeuvre. Presenting it in a roll makes it more unusual and attractive.

Cut two slices of brown bread ¼ inch (6 mm) thick, from the long side of a large loaf which is a day or two old. Trim off the crusts and place each slice on a sheet of kitchen wax paper or parchment. Spread the bread with softened butter, or substitute, and cover with the slices of salmon, overlapping as little as possible. Spread the horseradish down the center lengthwise and sprinkle generously with lemon juice and pepper. With the long edge nearest to you, using the wax paper as a support, roll up the bread as firmly as possible. Unwrap carefully from the paper and fix five cocktail sticks, evenly spaced, along the roll. Trim the ends with a sharp knife, and cut the roll into five pieces, making sure each one has a stick to hold it in place. Decorate with chives.

1 Cut two slices of bread, ¼" (6 mm) thick, from the long side of the loaf.

2 Place each on a sheet of wax paper and spread with butter, salmon, horseradish, lemon juice and pepper.

3 Roll up tightly along the longest side, using the paper as support.

4 Remove the paper. Fix roll with cocktail sticks, cut into five pieces and decorate.

FIG AND HAM ROLLS

Ingredients
3 fresh figs
1 oz (25 g) butter,
  softened
2 slices dried ham

There are many kinds of dried or smoked ham that can be eaten without further cooking. There is Parma and prosciutto from Italy, Bayonne from France, Westphalian from Germany and, from the U.S., Virginia or baked ham. All of these are usually sliced paper-thin, but for this recipe ask for the ham to be sliced a little thicker. If you are unable to get any of the dried or smoked products, a good, thinly-sliced boiled ham can be used, but it will have a much milder flavor.

Two slices of ham should be enough to make ten strips 2½ inches (6.5 cm) long and roughly ½ inch (1.5 cm) wide. The exact width of each strip will vary with the size of the figs, the ends of which should still be visible when the ham is wrapped around the center.

When figs are out of season, they can be replaced with a wide range of fruits – chunks of melon, pineapple and kiwi are all delicious.

1 *Spread the ham thinly with softened butter. Cut each slice into strips.*

2 *Cut the figs into quarters, lengthwise.*

3 *Roll the dried ham round the fig slices. Decorate with thyme flowers.*

SPICY AVOCADO AND TOMATO DIP

Ingredients

(makes about one cup
   of dip)
2 ripe avocados
2 Tbs lemon juice
4 canned tomatoes
2 tsp onion purée
½ tsp chili powder
Tabasco, to taste
salt and black pepper
cream, to taste
1 Tbs sugar, or to taste

This is a very flexible dip, which can be made as pungent or as mild as you like by adding more or less of the chili and Tabasco. If you want a completely different or milder flavor, these 'hot' ingredients can be omitted altogether, and soy, mushroom ketchup, chopped sun-dried tomatoes and some chopped herbs, such as basil, can be substituted either singly or in any combination.

Canned tomatoes vary considerably in size, but you will need about 6 oz (150 g) before sieving. They also vary in taste, and if they are very tart, more sugar can be added.

This dip, especially the milder version, is extremely suitable for fruit 'dippers', such as slices of apple, pear, banana or pineapple. The 'hot' version is more suited to vegetable crudités or crackers, as well as shrimps (prawns) on cocktail sticks.

1 *Sieve the tomatoes and add the lemon juice, onion purée and chili powder. Blend them together.*

2 *Halve the avocados, scoop out the flesh and add it to the blender. Blend the mixture again.*

3 *Thin to desired consistency with cream. Add Tabasco, salt, sugar and pepper, to taste.*

4 *Turn into a bowl and serve with assorted fruit, vegetables and crackers.*

STILTON AND CELERY BALLS

Ingredients
2½ oz (65 g) mild blue
  cheese
3½ oz (85 g) low fat soft
  cheese
1½ slices medium-thick
  white bread, a day or
  two old
2 sticks celery
1 Tbs brandy, or cream
½ oz (15 g) parsley,
  stalks removed
red pepper, for
  decoration

The surprise at coming across the crunchy celery in these creamy, tangy cheese balls usually gets people taking another one just to make sure of it. It is a good thing they are quick and easy to make.

Although any mild blue cheese can be used, French Rocquefort and English Stilton are undoubtedly the best for flavor. Unfortunately they are expensive, but as so little is required, it is worth using them if they are available. Do not make the balls more than ¾ inch (2 cm) in diameter, because in the absence of a cracker base the taste is quite strong.

The easiest way to make the celery pieces is to slit the sticks lengthwise in strips about ¼ inch (6 mm) wide and then, holding the bundle together, cut them across at ⅛ inch (3 mm) intervals.

The bread and parsley can be chopped together in a blender, but a more satisfactory coating is achieved when a herb mill or electric coffee grinder is used.

1 Chop the celery by cutting each stick lengthwise into strips and then across into small pieces.

2 Thoroughly mix the two cheeses, celery and brandy (or a little cream).

3 Cut crusts from the bread and make it into bread-crumbs. Grind the parsley and mix with the crumbs.

4 Make the mixture into small balls, roll in the breadcrumb mix. Decorate with small pepper shapes.

SALAMI CORNETS WITH BLUE CHEESE

Ingredients

5 slices salami
3 oz (75 g) low fat soft,
   or cream, cheese
1½ oz (40 g)
   well-ripened blue
   cheese
1 Tbs natural yogurt
1 tsp brandy
1 oz (25 g) butter,
   softened
green pepper, for
   decoration

These may not be the easiest of the hors d'oeuvres to prepare, but they look most professional. There is no difficulty in making the salami cornets, by overlapping the cut edges and fixing with a dab of soft butter, but filling them can be a little awkward.

Filling is best done by propping the cornet upright. A wire cake-rack, with spaces wide enough for the cones to stand vertically, can be useful.

It is not really necessary to use expensive blue cheeses such as French Rocquefort, English Stilton or Italian Gorganzola for this recipe, as there are plenty of good American and Danish ones. Be sure, however, that these are well ripened.

Any good spicy Italian sausage can be used instead of salami, but the slices must not be less than 3 inches (7.5 cm) in diameter.

1 *Cut the salami slices in half. Roll up to form cones and fix edges with a dab of soft butter.*

2 *Beat the cheeses, yogurt and brandy together to make a stiff cream.*

3 *Using a large nozzle, pipe the mixture into the cornets. Decorate with sticks of green pepper.*

SALMON AND BEET BOUCHEES

Ingredients

10 cocktail-size bouchée
  cases (see recipe p.11)
1 × 4 oz (100 g) can of
  salmon
1 Tbs cider or wine
  vinegar
sprinkling of cayenne
  pepper
1 Tbs mayonnaise
2 Tbs cooked beet
  (beetroot), chopped
freshly ground black
  pepper
chive flowers, for
  decoration

The crimson salmon and beet filling of these bouchées certainly adds a splash of color and gaiety to a table – and an unusual flavor to the tongue.

Tinned salmon is completely different from the fresh variety in both texture and taste, and each has its own distinct place in the culinary world. The flesh of tinned salmon is mildly sweet, and when mixed with beet, which has its own built-in sugar content, definitely needs the sharp contrast of vinegar. Be certain to use wine or cider vinegar, and not the harsh malt variety which is best left for pickles. If tinned or bottled beet are being used, check that they have been preserved in a mild vinegar or water. Always wear plastic gloves when chopping the beet as the vivid color, attractive though it may be, stains the fingers and nails.

After draining the salmon, remove the skin and at least the larger bones. Tease it apart with a fork, but do not mash, as this spoils the texture.

1 Chop the beet and put in a dish with a little vinegar.

2 Drain the salmon, put in a bowl and season with pepper and cayenne.

3 Fold in the mayonnaise, the chopped beet and the rest of the vinegar.

4 Fill the bouchée cases and decorate with chive flowers.

PISTACHIO AND SOFT CHEESE OLIVES

Ingredients
10 small pimento-stuffed olives
2 oz (50 g) low fat soft cheese
2 oz (50 g) chopped pistachio nuts
green pepper, for decoration

This is one of the quickest of all the hors d'oeuvres to prepare, but a food processor, nut mill, or even an electric coffee mill is important, as chopping nuts with a knife can be tedious.

Beat the cheese to a smooth paste and then cover each of the dried olives with a layer about ¼ inch (6 mm) thick. Roll this quickly between the palms of the hand to make a ball, which will take only a few seconds. After rolling in the chopped nuts, place in the fridge until needed.

Pistachio nuts are definitely the best, both for their flavor and their green color, which adds to the attraction of this hors d'oeuvre, but peanuts, hazelnuts or walnuts can be used. If larger stuffed olives are used, the finished balls can be cut in half to show concentric rings of red pimento, green olive, white cheese and green nuts.

1 *Shell the nuts. In a nut mill or food processor chop them until fine, but not powdered.*

2 *Drain and dry the olives, and cover each one with a heaped teaspoon of cheese.*

3 *Make each into a ball and roll in the chopped nuts until well covered. Decorate with sticks of green pepper.*

CHERRY TOMATOES WITH FETA CHEESE AND OLIVES

Ingredients
10 cherry tomatoes
3 oz (75 g) feta cheese
10 small black olives
1 tsp wine or balsamic
  vinegar
salt and freshly ground
  black pepper

Feta is a Greek low-fat cheese made from sheeps' or goats' milk, with a light crumbly texture.
It combines perfectly with tomatoes and olives which is why the three are used together so widely in Greek cookery.

Use a fine saw-edged knife to cut the tops from the tomatoes, scooping out and discarding the seeds. Sprinkle the insides with salt, then turn upside down to drain for a few minutes before seasoning with pepper and a few drops of balsamic vinegar (the diluted versions available in most supermarkets are quite satisfactory).

Choose small black olives which have much more flavor than the larger ones, and when filling the tomatoes, pile the cheese high above the rim to obtain the full decorative effect.

1 *Cut the tops from the tomatoes, scoop out the seeds, sprinkle inside with salt and turn upside down to drain.*

2 *Cut the tops from the black olives for decoration. Chop the remainder and mix with the feta cheese.*

3 *Dry the insides of the tomatoes with kitchen paper and season with black pepper and a drop of balsamic vinegar.*

4 *Fill with the feta and olive mixture, using the olive tops for decoration.*

3
SPECIAL OCCASION
HORS D'OEUVRES

PRUNES WITH PICKLED WALNUT AND CHEESE STUFFING

Ingredients
10 large prunes
3 oz (75 g) cream cheese
5 pickled walnuts, chopped
orange wedges, for decoration

These are among the simplest hors d'oeuvres and can be made in five minutes with no difficulty. Most people find the contrast between the sweetish prunes and the sharp tangy taste of the pickled walnuts particularly enjoyable.

Use the biggest and best prunes you can get, preferably tenderized ones. The French consider that their prunes d'Agen are the best in the world, but this would be disputed by California growers. Pour boiling water over them to plump them a little while you blend together the cream cheese and the finely-chopped walnuts. If the mixture is too stiff add a little of the pickle liquid. When you have stuffed the prunes, decorate them with a wedge of orange with the skin still attached. Serve on cocktail sticks, stuck diagonally through the prunes.

1 *Mix the cream cheese together with the finely-chopped pickled walnuts.*

2 *Drain the prunes in a sieve. Dry on kitchen paper and pit them.*

3 *Stuff the prunes with a good teaspoonful of the mixture, and decorate with trimmed orange pieces.*

HORSERADISH AND EGG CRACKERS

Ingredients
10 small, round crackers
2/3 eggs, hard-boiled
1 oz butter, softened
2 tsp creamed
  horseradish
cocktail gherkins, for
  decoration
radishes, for decoration

All food should look attractive, and this applies especially to hors d'oeuvres. This one, though simple, usually brings exclamations of delight for its appearance.

Hard-boiled eggs are very easy, and when cooked properly are delicious, but when sliced they are sometimes spoiled visually by the yolk not being central in the white. To achieve this, keep the eggs upright while cooking – by wedging the fiber container, in which they are normally bought, in the bottom of a pan and replacing the eggs, point down. Cover them with cold water, bring to the boil and simmer for ten minutes. Pour off the hot water, run in cold for 30 seconds and then allow the eggs to stand in the water until cool enough to handle. Remove the shells and place the eggs in fresh cold water until needed.

1 *Beat the softened butter and horseradish together. Spread it on the crackers.*

2 *Cut the eggs into slices about ¼" (6 mm) thick, and put a slice on each cracker.*

3 *Decorate with gherkins and radishes, as desired.*

ARTICHOKE HEARTS WITH CAVIAR AND CREAM CHEESE

Ingredients
10 artichoke hearts
3 oz (75 g) cream cheese
3 oz (75 g) cottage
  cheese
4 oz (100 g) red caviar
  or lumpfish roe
1 oz (25 g) black caviar
  or lumpfish roe

Though this may sound like a recipe for a grand party, it is really quite simple and relatively cheap. Small, whole, tinned artichokes are widely available and are surprisingly good in view of the fact that many vegetables lose their flavor in canning. Lumpfish roe, which is usually in jars, is a perfectly satisfactory substitute for the extremely expensive *real* caviar,

The fish eggs should be washed to prevent color 'bleeding' into the cheese, and this must be done very carefully as they break easily (see page 70). Likewise great care should be used when folding the roe into the cheese mixture.

In order to hold the filling, it may be necessary to enlarge the cavity in the artichoke hearts by removing some of the inner leaves, but these can be chopped and added to the cheese and 'caviar' mix.

1 Drain the artichoke hearts in a sieve, cutting the bases so that they stand level.

2 Turn first the red and then the black 'caviar' into a sieve and wash carefully. Drain and dry gently.

3 Beat together the cheeses and fold in, extremely carefully, 3 oz (75 g) of the red 'caviar'.

4 Dry the artichokes and fill with the mixture. Sprinkle with red and black fish eggs.

SALAMI BUNDLES

Ingredients
10 slices salami
2 dill pickles
½ yellow pepper
½ red pepper
2 carrots

When the table fork was introduced to England from Italy in about 1600, one angry writer, regretting the imminent passing of the old finger-feasting, thundered 'Who would make hay of his food and pitch it into his mouth with a fork?'
This recipe with its bundles of vegetation, although definitely finger-feeding, does perhaps resemble pitching bundles of hay into the mouth.

Hungarian salami is very good for this recipe because of its excellent flavor, but any other salami will do as long as it is not more than 3 inches (7.5 cm) in diameter.

Almost any crisp crunchy vegetable can be used, provided it is brightly colored, but dill cucumbers should always be included to give a sharpness to offset the salty, oily flavor of the salami.

The vegetables should be cut into sticks ⅛ × 3 inches (3 × 75 mm), although it may be difficult to get the pepper as thin as this.

1 *Slice the vegetables lengthwise into matchsticks.*

2 *On each salami slice place an assortment of the vegetable matchsticks.*

3 *Roll the salami tightly round the vegetables and fasten with a cocktail stick.*

AVOCADO AND LIME CRACKERS

Ingredients
10 crackers
1 ripe avocado
juice of 1 lime
½ oz (15 g) butter
1 Tbs chopped green
 herbs
¼ tsp cayenne pepper
salt and black pepper
10 medium-size shrimps
 (prawns) shelled, fresh
 or frozen

This is an easily-prepared and delicious hors d'oeuvre, but much depends on selecting the avocado. An under-ripe one will be hard, chewy and tasteless, while an over-ripe one will have discolored mushy flesh. When choosing one, look for a large fruit which is firm, but not hard: it should 'give' slightly when pressed, and the stalk end should be a darker green. Hass avocados have a thick, rough skin, almost black in color and are apparently quite hard. They are ripe if the stalk end is dried up.

The addition of lime juice to the avocado is not only to give a sharp flavor to contrast with the buttery flesh, but also to prevent the purée discoloring rapidly to a dirty gray. For this reason it is better to put the lime juice into your mixing bowl first and mash the avocado into it.

The easiest way to chop the herbs is in a herb mill. Here we have used parsley and chervil.

1 *Chop the herbs and beat into the softened butter.*

2 *Spread the herb butter thinly onto the crackers*

3 *Mash the avocado flesh with all of the lime juice and season to taste.*

4 *Pile the avocado purée on each cracker and top with a prawn which has been sprinkled with cayenne.*

CELERY BITES WITH ORANGE, CHEESE AND RAISINS

Ingredients

3 – 4 sticks of celery
3 oz (75 g) cream cheese
3 oz (75 g) Cheddar cheese
2 oz (50 g) raisins
3 Tbs rum, orange liqueur, or orange juice
1 small orange
1 Tbs finely chopped chives or scallions

Most hors d'oeuvres are savory or even spicy: this one is definitely sweet, with its orange flesh and rum-soaked raisins combining with the cream cheese to make a filling which would not be out of place in a cheesecake.

As the top end of the celery stick is narrow and the bottom wide (giving respectively too little and too much stuffing in proportion to the celery flesh) it is better to use the central part of the stalk only. Trimming the underneath of the celery pieces will make them stand level on the dish.

If you can put the raisins to soak in the rum, orange liqueur or juice for an hour or two before they are needed, their texture and flavor will be greatly improved. The orange taste will also be much stronger if the finely-grated zest from the orange is mixed into the cheese.

1 Cut two ½" (1.5 cm) slices of the orange. Cut off the peel and pith. Remove flesh in segments.

2 Mix together the cheeses, raisins, rum and orange flesh, keeping aside ten pieces for decoration.

3 Fill about 15" (38 cm) of the celery sticks with the mixture.

4 Cut into 1½" (4 cm) pieces and decorate with orange segments and raisins.

CUCUMBER CUPS OF PATE

Ingredients
1 straight piece of
  cucumber, about 5"
  (13 cm) long
4 oz (100 g) duck liver
  pâté
1 small orange
1 tsp fresh orange juice
  or liqueur
salt

The crisp cucumber cups contrast well here with the softer liver and orange pâté filling, and a teaspoon of liqueur such as Cointreau or Grand Marnier added to the pâté mixture will enhance the flavor. Although duck is used in this recipe, chicken liver pâté would do equally well.

The quickest way to scoop out the hollows in the cucumber pieces is to use a serrated grapefruit knife, but a teaspoon can be used. Take care not to cut through the base of each cup, though small slits are not important as the filling is quite stiff. The cups must be dried well, inside and out, before filling, or the watery juice will spoil the pâté.

The neatest way of putting the pâté into the cups is to use a piping bag with a large, ¾ inch (2 cm) nozzle, but two teaspoons can be used if the pâté is not fine enough to pipe.

1 Cut slices of cucumber ½" (1.5 cm) thick. Scoop out a hollow in each. Sprinkle in some salt. Drain and dry.

2 Grate the zest from ⅔ of the orange, saving ⅓ of the peel for decoration. Squeeze out the juice.

3 Mash the pâté with the orange zest, and then add the orange juice.

4 Pipe the pâté into the cucumber. Decorate with orange and cucumber shapes cut from the skins.

SMOKED SALMON BARQUETTES (LITTLE BOATS)

Ingredients

10 barquette cases (see recipe p.11)
6 oz (150 g) cream cheese
1 slice thickly cut smoked salmon
2 Tbs caviar or black lumpfish roe
lemon juice and freshly ground black pepper, to taste
lemon slices, for decoration

Smoked salmon and caviar sounds extravagant, but the quantities used in this recipe are so small that the cost is quite low. The salmon slice must be about 5 × 3 inches (12.5 × 7.5 cm); genuine Russian caviar is exorbitantly expensive, but black lumpfish roe is more than adequate.

The individual eggs in the fish roe are very fragile. Take the roe from the jar into a sieve and wash in a bowl or under gently running water. Drain and dry thoroughly with paper towels or a soft cloth.

If you cannot buy the boat-shaped barquettes and haven't time to make them (see recipe p.11), any of the long, narrow or diamond-shaped pastry cases available in delicatessens will do.

For the ultimate party, lightly-smoked wild Norwegian salmon with Caspian Beluga caviar will make an hors d'oeuvre never to be forgotten.

1 Cut 20 small triangles of salmon to cover the ends of the barquettes. Keep aside.

2 Mix the cream cheese, lemon juice, black pepper and salmon trimmings. Fill the barquettes.

3 Spoon a band of roe across the center of the filling. Cover the ends with the salmon triangles.

4 Cut slices of lemon peel, with a little of the flesh remaining, and place on the roe, across the center.

4
Hot
Hors D'oeuvres

GRILLED PRUNE AND BACON ROLLS

Ingredients
10 tenderized prunes
10 Jordan almonds, not skinned
10 rashers streaky bacon, 7 – 8" (18 – 20 cm) long

Sometimes this recipe is called 'Devils-on-Horseback' to contrast, I suppose, with the more usual grilled oysters wrapped in bacon generally known as 'Angels-on-Horseback'. I cannot suggest any reason for the name unless it is that while oysters might be considered white and therefore, traditionally, pure; prunes are definitely black and therefore, supposedly, evil.

In view of the fact that I have seen many guests surreptitiously removing the almonds in the belief that they are the prune pits, it is as well either to label this hors d'oeuvre or to tell people beforehand that they are stuffed.

As with all cooked hors d'oeuvres, soak the cocktail sticks in water for an hour or two to prevent charring. If the pieces are being grilled, do not forget to turn them several times.

1 *Pour boiling water over the prunes and leave to stand for a few minutes.*

2 *Pit the prunes using a sharp knife and replace the stones with almonds.*

3 *Wrap the bacon round the prunes, secure with cocktail sticks and cook in the oven or grill until the bacon is done.*

CROUSTADES OF SMOKED MEAT

Ingredients

10 croustades (see
    recipe p. 10)
4 oz (100 g) pastrami,
    roughly chopped
5 pickled walnuts,
    chopped
1 tsp mild mustard
1 Tbs mayonnaise

Home-made croustades (oven-baked bread cases) with their golden crunchy 'toast' are an unusual base for hors d'oeuvres. If you do not wish to make them, they can be bought in specialty shops, but are often smaller and made of a wafer-like crust.

An alternative to croustades are tartlet cases, which also can be home-made or bought. The recipes for both of these are on pages 10 and 11.

Kassler or any other cooked, smoked meat can be used and chopped coarsely or more finely. Capers can be used instead of pickled walnuts.

Until fifty years ago, many people who had a walnut tree in their garden made their own pickled walnuts. The nuts were picked long before they were ripe, when the shells were still soft and green. They were then pierced with a knitting needle, soaked in brine for twelve days and exposed to sunlight, which turned them black. They were then sealed tightly in jars of vinegar.

1 *In a food processor, chop the meat with the mustard. Turn into a bowl.*

2 *Mix the mayonnaise and pickled walnuts in with the meat.*

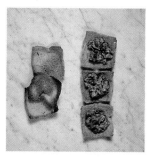

3 *Pile the mixture into the croustades and heat in a moderate oven (350°F/180°C/Mark 4).*

TOASTED CHEESE ROLLS

Ingredients

2 long slices bread, one
  or two days old
1½ oz (40 g) butter,
  melted
3 Tbs tomato ketchup
3 oz (75 g) Cheddar
  cheese, finely grated
sprinkling of paprika
2 sheets wax paper

To look and taste their best, these hors d'oeuvre should be served as soon as they are taken from the oven, with the melted cheese bubbling up from the crisp golden roll.

Soak the cocktail sticks in water for several hours before use or they may char in the oven.

The bread must be one or two days old, as a fresh loaf will be difficult to cut into ¼ inch (6 mm) slices and anything thicker may crack when rolled. Wholemeal bread can be used, but it must be made from finely-ground flour without whole grains. The bread slices are cut from the long side of the loaf and should be about 7 × 5 inches (18 × 12.5 cm) before the crusts are removed. Use a strongly-flavored tomato ketchup and a mature, tasty hard cheese such as Cheddar for the best results.

When the rolls are in the oven turn them frequently and remove as soon as they are sizzling.

1 *Remove the crusts from the bread slices. Spread melted butter sparingly on both sides.*

2 *Place the bread slices on sheets of wax paper. Spread with ketchup, grate on the cheese and sprinkle with paprika.*

3 *Roll up the bread tightly, starting from the long side. Use the kitchen parchment to support it, then remove.*

4 *Fix the roll with cocktail sticks. Cut into 1½ inch (4 cm) lengths and bake at (350°C/180°C/Mark 4), until golden.*

STUFFED CURRIED MUSHROOMS

Ingredients

10 cupped mushrooms
1 tsp puréed or grated onion
2 Tbs chutney
1 tsp curry powder
sprinkling of paprika
3 oz (75 g) Cheddar cheese

This recipe can be adjusted to suit the average guest who enjoys just a slight tangy tingle, or the red-hot curry addict with toughened tastebuds.

Mushrooms are very variable, and you should choose those which are firm and fleshy in texture, slightly cupped in shape and about 1½ inches (4 cm) in diameter. If you can get only the thinner, flatter ones, you may have to serve them on a round base such as corn wafers, crackers or toasts. To make sure the mushrooms stand level and firm, you may need to trim the rounded bottoms.

Tubes of puréed onion can be bought, but a little grated mild onion can be used if you prefer. Curried chutney is usually available, but if it is not, or if you prefer a more powerful mixture, use any chutney pepped up with curry powder to your taste. Start off with about 1 teaspoonful, increasing until the mixture reaches the desired strength.

Any hard cheese can be used in this recipe.

1 Remove the stems from the mushrooms. Place the caps in a bowl, and pour boiling water over them. Leave them to stand.

2 Mix together the chutney, onion, curry powder and paprika. Grate the cheese and stir 2 oz (50 g) of it into the mixture.

3 Drain the mushrooms in a sieve, and dry well on kitchen paper.

4 Heap the mixture on the caps and top with the remaining grated cheese. Grill until the cheese is bubbling.

TOMATOES FILLED WITH DEVILED CRAB

Ingredients
10 small tomatoes
6 oz (150 g) mixed crab
1½ oz (40 g) butter
3 – 4 Tbs cream
2 Tbs fine breadcrumbs
1½ Tbs grated cheese
1½ Tbs brandy
salt and black pepper

Deviling mixture
1 tsp mild mustard
1 Tbs chopped chives or
　scallions
dash Worcestershire
　sauce
dash Tabasco
2 tsp cayenne pepper

Use fresh crab, if you can get it, as it has more flavor and can be tasted even through the deviling mixture. Frozen crab is a good substitute when the white and brown meats are combined, but canned crab is not recommended.

The mixture can be piled into the warm tomato cases, decorated quickly with borage blossoms, when in flower, or sprigs of dill or parsley. Serve immediately.

Alternatively, this hors d'oeuvre can be made several hours in advance. To do this, cook the mixture and keep it in the fridge until fifteen minutes before it is needed. Then fill the tomato cases and warm in a moderate oven for about ten minutes.

1 Cut tops from the tomatoes. Scoop out the seeds. Drain and warm very gently in the oven.

2 Melt the butter and cook the crab gently for a minute. Add breadcrumbs, cream and 'deviling' ingredients.

3 Stir constantly until thick and creamy, but not dry. Taste and adjust seasoning. Add the cheese and brandy.

4 Pile the mixture into the warm tomato cases, decorate and serve hot.

SHRIMP AND OLIVE STICKS

Ingredients
10 large shrimps
  (prawns), shelled
10 black olives, pitted,
  or 10 green pimento-
  stuffed olives
1 oz (25 g) butter, melted
10 cocktail sticks
sprinkling of cayenne
  pepper or paprika

This hors d'oeuvre is so quick and easy that it scarcely needs a recipe.

The small olives have much more flavor than the larger ones, and the black fruit contrasts well with the pink shrimps. Buy shrimps which are large enough to curl round the olives – the packs of frozen ones are very good.

You will probably need to start with more than ten shrimps as invariably some break when you try to put them on the cocktail sticks. The most difficult part of the operation is ensuring that the stick passes firmly through the olive and both ends of the fish. If they are not secure they may come apart during cooking. Cayenne pepper sprinkled over the shrimp immediately before serving deepens the pink color, but if you do not want a spicy taste, mild paprika has the same effect.

1 *Curl a shrimp round each olive and push a pre-soaked cocktail stick through both.*

2 *Brush the shrimps gently with a little melted butter on both sides.*

3 *Grill on both sides under a hot grill, and place on kitchen paper to absorb any surplus fat.*

GOAT CHEESE TOASTS

Ingredients

2 medium-thick slices of
  bread
½ oz (15 g) butter,
  softened
2 oz (50 g) mild goat
  cheese
1 oz (25 g) sun-dried
  tomatoes in oil,
  chopped
1 Tbs tomato ketchup
1 tsp chopped basil or
  oregano
cherry tomatoes, for
  decoration

Normally bread is toasted first and then buttered, but for hors d'oeuvres it is often buttered before being toasted to give a crisper texture.

Goat cheeses are very variable, so when shopping look for one which is fresh and mild, but not tasteless. Staler ones will have a smell of ammonia. Sun-dried tomatoes in oil are consistent in quality and though they are expensive they have a unique flavor. In this recipe, tomato purée can be used as a substitute, but the result will be quite different.

If you cannot get fresh basil or oregano, parsley can be used instead, but basil or oregano, with their strong Mediterranean overtones, are particularly good with any tomato dish.

The goat cheese and ketchup will mash together very easily, but it will probably be necessary to snip the sun-dried tomatoes into small pieces before beating them and the herbs into the mixture.

Serve very hot.

1 *Remove the crusts from the bread. Spread very thinly with butter on one side only, and toast.*

2 *Mash the goat cheese, ketchup, herbs and sun-dried tomatoes, and spread on buttered side of toast.*

3 *Grill until very hot. Cut the toast into triangles and decorate with cherry tomato quarters.*

INDEX